Because of H.E.R.

By Jamilah F. Bashir, M.Ed.

<u>Acknowledgements</u>

I would like to thank Allah (God) for allowing me to produce this book. It was a true labor of love. I have to thank my family and friends for their support, especially my mom. During the creation of this book she had to discuss some events from her past that was difficult for her. I am very grateful she had the strength to do it. Ameenah Muhammad-Diggins and Halimah Deoliveira for sparking the fire in me to write a book. Both of their motivation and guidance truly helped me to create this book. Michelle Grier for editing my book and helping me with my book signing. I appreciate your support and how our editing sessions turned into life conversations with plenty of laughter. My accountability partners, you know who you are. I truly appreciate the check-ins and encouragement throughout this process. Aliya Khabir for her support and helping me to not overwhelm myself. I have to give a tremendous thank you to my sister Taaliba Dunbar. She has been by my side supporting me since I first had the idea to write a book and never left. Not once did she discourage me, but has uplifted me and I am forever grateful to have her in my life. I love you to the moon and back. Last but certainly not least, my sister Aasiyah Bashir. She is the driving force behind Because of H.E.R. and has had a huge impact on my life. Without her, there would be no book and I would not be teaching. I love you dearly.

Jamilah F. Bashir, M.Ed.

Before

H.E.R.

Because of H.E.R

"Okay, I need to get taco shells, salsa, shredded cheese, sour cream, lettuce, and red onions," I said aloud as I pushed the red shopping cart down the aisle. "Mmmm tacos, you're gonna eat good tonight," Aasiyah (Ah-Se-Ya) said with a huge smile on her face. Remembering that I needed to buy paper towel, I made a sudden stop with the cart. "Aasiyah, watch the cart and my purse, I'm going over to that aisle to get paper towel," I said while pointing to the exact aisle, reassuring her that I wasn't going far. I darted toward the aisle for the paper towel, grabbed the pack that I needed and headed back to my sister and our shopping cart. As soon as I turned toward my sister's direction, I saw a woman dressed in black clothing talking to her. The woman was standing close to our cart, close to where my purse was sitting. My eyes widened and I had a bad feeling in my stomach. I thought to myself, "who is this woman and why is she talking to my sister? She better not try distracting my sister to steal money from my purse." I immediately shouted, "Can I help you?" The woman and my

sister were startled, quickly turning in my direction. I have never moved so fast from one place to the next. Before the woman could respond, I had gently pushed my sister and our cart aside and I stood directly in front of the woman. Aasiyah did not question me once about moving her or why I was coming off concerned with this woman. Her reaction stemmed from our mother expressing how much she did not tolerate siblings disrespecting each other. Especially, with older siblings. Again, I asked, "Can I help you?" The woman replied that she had fallen on hard times and wanted to know if we could spare some money, so she could buy groceries. I politely asked her to wait where she stood. I grabbed Aasiyah's hand and pushed the cart further down the aisle to prevent her from seeing how much cash I was carrying in my wallet. After checking my purse to ensure nothing was missing, I went into my wallet for money to give the woman. I walked up the aisle and kindly placed the money in her hand. The woman thanked us for our kind deed, then walked away. I headed back to where my sister stood and with much frustration.

I said, "You can't just talk to strangers Aasiyah! Everyone is not nice, you can't trust everyone! I keep telling you this!".

"I'm sorry", she replied.

"Aasiyah you have to be careful," I complained.

She looked like she was going to cry and I immediately hugged her. It's hard for her to understand what I mean because she sees the good in everyone. Aasiyah must learn these lessons because I am not going to be around all the time to protect her. My sister, Aasiyah, isn't like everyone else. She's different.

I am part of a blended family, with six daughters. Amongst my sisters I come in at number five, next to the youngest. I wasn't raised with all my sisters. Three of my sisters lived with their mother and would visit occasionally. I was raised with my big sister Taaliba (Ta-lee-ba), my mom's daughter from a previous marriage, and my little sister Aasiyah. At the age of six, when my parents told me that Mom was pregnant, I was elated. I can remember thinking, "I'll finally have a little brother." To my surprise, months into her pregnancy Mom discovered that she was having a girl. Initially I was crushed because I really wanted a little brother. However, I got over my disappointment because I was excited that I would be someone's big sister.

On August 16, 1991, my little sister Aasiyah was born. She did not weigh enough at birth so she had to stay in the hospital for a while until she gained enough weight to come home. I remember Mom being extremely sad because my sister couldn't come home right away. Being only six years old, I didn't understand why my mom would stay in her room and cry. I could easily understand that she wanted my sister home, what mother wouldn't want their newborn home with them? Yet, being so young I didn't know my mom was suffering from what they now call Postpartum Depression. Postpartum Depression occurs in some women after the birth of a child. They experience an overwhelming sadness and feeling of not being able

to adequately be a mother. I remember an influx of my mom's friends visiting her to lift her spirits while my sister was in the hospital. These constant visits really helped her get through her Postpartum Depression.

The day Aasiyah was coming home I was overjoyed! I chose the outfit she was going to wear home. I chose a onesie that was covered in pastel shades of mint green and blush pink. The onesie also had little flowers on it. I repeatedly asked my parents, "Is it time yet for you to go and get Aasiyah?" I could not wait to hold my sister.

My sister Taaliba and I stayed home while my parents went to retrieve Aasiyah from the hospital. I sat patiently by the big window in our living room, waiting for my parents' car to pull up in front of the house. The window was wide with white lace curtains hanging from both sides. Our house was close to the corner and the window faced the street. We could easily see when my Dad's car would turn onto our block.

Finally, I saw the front of my dad's grey Ford

Pinto turning the corner. I shouted at the top of my lungs, "They're Here"! My sister rushed to the door, unlocking it. We stood at the screen door waiting for our parents to walk inside. Our excitement was bubbling over as we watched our parents stop at two of our neighbors' houses before coming inside.

When my parents finally walked inside, my sister and I ran to Mom for a glance at our new baby sister. We ran so fast to our parents that we nearly knocked them over in excitement. As I looked at my sister I thought, "I wanted a brother, but I guess she'll do." She had beautiful smooth brown skin and a head full of curly soft hair. The wait was finally over, Aasiyah was home.

My little sister, Aasiyah, was a sweet and loving addition to our family. However, between the ages of nine and twelve months, Mom noticed that my sister was not growing and developing at the same rate as Taaliba and I had when we were younger. She decided to visit Aasiyah's pediatrician with her concerns. Surprisingly, the doctor didn't notice anything alarming, assuring Mom that my sister would eventually meet her milestones. Since the doctor showed no concern, Mom accepted the doctor's advice and thought, "maybe Aasiyah is just taking her time, in due to time she will show us what she can do."

As time went on, although achieving these milestones late in her development, Aasiyah learned to sit up on her own, crawl, and walk. Nonetheless, she did not talk as much and she often used her hands to show people what she wanted and needed. Aasiyah, at that time, was almost two years old and again not hitting milestones the same as other children her age. It was then that Mom learned that my sister would have limitations due to her slow cognitive development, which at the time was called mental retardation. It is now called an intellectual disability.

There is no one specific cause of an intellectual disability. A woman having problems during her pregnancy or complications during the birth of a child could contribute to the child having an intellectual disability. Being only six years old I did not understand what my mom meant when she said my sister would have problems. In my eyes she looked and acted fine to me. As Aasiyah grew up I noticed that she had trouble climbing the stairs and her movements were not the normal movements of someone going up a flight of stairs. She did not climb the steps like one foot on one step and then push off to place her other foot on the next step. She would lose her balance while walking up the steps. Aasiyah would always hold onto the railing on the stairs, going step by step to climb the stairs. In other words, she would place her foot on a step and then place her other foot on that same step, then place one foot on the next step and then place her other foot on the same step. She also had difficulty drinking through a straw. She would try her best, but she struggled to fix her mouth and lips on the straw to drink. Tying her shoes was another obstacle. Aasiyah could not maneuver her fingers into the different positions to tie her shoes. If she had shoes that needed to be tied, I would tie them for her or she would stuff them down in her shoe.

This was very frustrating for me because I would get tired of having to tie her shoes for her. Aasiyah continued to have a hard time remembering how to tie her shoes on her own. At times when we would get ready to leave the house, I would lean my head back and sigh, "ugh". I thought to myself, "Here we go again with tying these shoes". Eventually, Mom stopped buying shoes with laces. She felt Velcro straps or slip on shoes would be easier for Aasiyah to manage. Another struggle for Aasiyah was buttoning or zipping up her clothes. She could not pull buttons through their adjacent hole. To zipper her pants, I had to button the top of her pants, holding them in place for her to pull the zipper up to the top. For her coat, Mom tied string at the end of her zipper to make it easier for her to pull her zipper up or down. Additionally, Aasiyah's speech was not clear. When she talked it sounded like she was holding spit in her mouth. Often, I would say, "Aasiyah, swallow that spit, then talk and speak up." Being an older sibling, you never think that your baby sister or brother would have limitations with simple tasks like walking upstairs or getting dressed.

I never imagined that my little sister would have obstacles keeping her from living a "normal" life. Little did I know, she would have such a huge impact on my life. I now felt like I had to be my sister's protector. This was new for me being as though I was the youngest child for six years. I felt like I had to protect my sister from those who did not and could not understand that she had a disability. I would be lying if I said that I did not feel embarrassed by my little sister. Initially, I did because I often had to explain to people why my sister could not do certain tasks on her own. I had to deal with ignorant comments like, "her sister must be slow or something" or "she must be retarded."

Once, when my sister and I were attending a community event, Aasiyah was about six years old and I was twelve. We went over to an arts and crafts activity area where we could draw, color pictures, make crafts, etc. Aasiyah chose to color a picture. There were other children in the area doing crafts as well. A girl saw Aasiyah's picture and loudly asked, "Why you color like that?" Aasiyah's picture looked sloppy because she had trouble staying in the lines when she colored. I could see the other children heads turning to look at Aasiyah's picture and all eyes were on her. I felt so embarrassed and wanted to just erase this moment from happening. Nevertheless, I wasn't going to allow my sister to be the center of attention. I looked at the girl who made the announcement about Aasiyah's picture and said, "Yours don't look that much better than hers, why do you care?" The girl got quiet and went back to coloring. A few of the other children laughed and Aasiyah grabbed her picture and we left. Moments like that forced me to shy away from being out with my sister because I felt that it was too much to deal with. So often, I wanted to stay home because our home felt like a safe-haven. I didn't have to deal with people's questions or mean comments. When we were out in public I was always on-edge and on-guard. I would try to play with friends, but I would have to make sure my sister was okay, and no one was bothering her.

During Aasiyah's toddler years, she attended Kencrest. Kencrest is an agency that works with individuals with disabilities. Once, while at Kencrest, a psychologist had to observe and evaluate Aasiyah's social and motor skills. I was not present for this observation, but I remember seeing Mom upset and hurt when she returned. Mom said that after my sister's observation, the Psychologist reviewed the notes with her and Aasiyah's teachers. The Psychologist told my mom that Aasiyah would be unable to communicate verbally. Aasiyah needed a special keyboard to assist her with communicating. I remember thinking, "A keyboard? She talks all the time. It's getting her to shut up that's difficult." I was amused by the thought. The Psychologist also shared that my sister could not drink from a straw and her balance was off. It was hard for my mom to digest the Psychologists' results of my sister's evaluation. What mother wants to hear that something is wrong with their child? I can remember my mom feeling defeated, blaming herself for my sister's disability. Although feeling hurt and guilt, Mom knew that my sister could perform every task the psychologist said that she could not perform. Mom also knew that Aasiyah would mimic everything that I did. So, Mom asked the Psychologist to perform another observation, permitting me to tag along. The day of the observation, my mom, Aasiyah, the Psychologist, Aasiyah's teacher, and I went to a room that looked a lot like Aasiyah's classroom. The floor had brown carpeting and there were different stations in the room, each with small tables and chairs. There was an area with a kitchen play-set and food. There was also an area with books and puppets. That area had a large colorful area rug covered with the alphabet and numbers. In the dress-up area, there were block mazes sitting on shelves. The mazes were twistable blocks strung along thin metal poles. Every Pediatrician has those block mazes in their office waiting area. I was extremely excited that Mom brought me along with her to Aasiyah's observation. In the room, Aasiyah and I sat at one of the miniature dining tables with two cups filled with water and a straw. Everything the Psychologist asked my sister to do I would do it first, and Aasiyah would follow right after me. The Psychologist saw that my sister was talking with me, she drank from a straw, and climbed stairs to go down the sliding board. In my mind, I was screamed, "Go Aasi it's your birthday, Go Aasi it's your birthday!"

Aasiyah was proving to the Psychologist that she in fact, could perform everything that she said she could not. For the first time I was proud and not embarrassed to be Aasiyah's big sister. I did not realize this until I was older, but she looked up to me and I was her example of how to behave and maneuver in the world. In her eyes, I was what she wanted to be. From this new observation, the Psychologist had to revise her report. I had no idea how Aasiyah was implanting seeds in me that would later guide me to a line of work that I never saw myself doing.

As we got older, I had a hard time trusting people around my sister. My distrust derived from wanting to determine whether people were genuine or looking to make fun of her. Growing up with a sibling that has an intellectual disability had its challenges. Having a younger sister like Aasiyah caused me to be more protective of her than a normal big sister would. If anyone bothered my little sister, I would immediately go to an angry dark place and feel enraged, ready to beat anybody down for bothering her.

There was a time when Aasiyah and I were at the mall when a boy, who looked older than Aasiyah but younger than me, said something mean to my sister. He was making fun of Aasiyah. He was secretly pointing at her and laughing to his friends standing next to him. Aasiyah did not realize the boy was making fun of her, but I did. I then grabbed Aasiyah's arm, stomping away. I was not going to keep her there allowing him to make fun of her. We left and waited outside for our mom to come out so that we could go home. When we were outside, I noticed the same boy who made fun of Aasiyah came outside as well. Once we made it outside, he walked past Aasiyah and I, laughing. At that moment I was furious. I felt my fury rise from the bottom of my feet, up to the top of my head. I looked at him with tunnel vision. I saw nothing but him. I immediately snapped back and harshly said, "what's so funny?". My facial expression read, "I know what you were doing!" The boy's eyes were as big as saucers as he nervously replied, "nothing." I took Aasiyah's hand and we walked away, waiting for Mom by her car. My goodness, I was so angry that I wanted to punch that boy in his face. This time I wasn't just angry, I was also hurt. Aasiyah had no idea the boy was making fun of her and if she had known she didn't know how to reply.

How dare he make fun of someone that can't defend herself? As a matter of fact, how dare he sit and make fun of anyone? That is one of the meanest things you can do to a person. I felt hurt that he thought it was okay to sit and make fun of my sister. I didn't want NOBODY bothering my sister. As a result, I became extremely overprotective of Aasiyah. If I didn't know who you were, I didn't want you talking to or being around my sister. At times even if I knew you, my attitude was always, "like what do you want with my sister."

Because of H.E.R

Jamilah F. Bashir, M.Ed.

After

H.E.R.

Because of H.E.R

Growing up I always wanted a career in the medical field. I loved science and I also wanted to make good money. My dream was to become a neurosurgeon until I decided that I wanted to be a pediatrician instead. Therefore, when I attended college at Widener University, I majored in Biology with a concentration in Pre-Medicine. I loved every biology class, but chemistry was killing me, whooping my behind, UGH!!!! So, I then decided to change my major while keeping my pre-medicine concentration. One afternoon, my friend and I were flipping through the degree program catalog in hopes of finding a new major for me.

"What about social work?", asked my friend.

"No," I replied. "I don't want to do that."

"What about engineering?"

"No, I'm not into that either"

I continued flipping through the catalog until I reached the Education section.

My friend shouted, "oooooh you can be a teacher!"

My face immediately frowned.

"I don't want to deal with these bad behind kids!" I replied with an attitude.

I turned the page and saw Special Education.

"Special Education", I said aloud.

"Do that!!" replied my friend. "You can work with children that are disabled" As soon as she said that, I immediately thought of my little sister Aasiyah and other children like her.

"I could make a difference and my sister needs a teacher that truly cares" I thought to myself.

So, I changed my major to Special Education, but I kept my pre-medicine concentration because I wasn't ready to give up on my dream of having a career in the medical field. Wow! I couldn't believe how much I enjoyed my education and psychology courses. I also enjoyed one of the science courses I needed to fulfill my pre-medicine requirements. I began to fall in love with my new major.

"Did I really want to be a teacher?" I asked myself.

Although I was thrilled with the Special Education curriculum I still struggled with making a final decision on my career path.

Later that year, I took a work study job at a local elementary school near Widener's campus. There I was, a tutor in one of their Special Education classrooms. I TRULY enjoyed that experience. "What is happening to me? I don't really want to be a teacher," I said to myself. Then I started thinking about Aasiyah and how she and other children like her deserve quality and caring educators. They especially need more educators of color who looked like them. I started to feel as if a calling was being put on me to become a Special Education teacher. However, I kept fighting it. It felt like a game of tug of war was going on inside me. I was being pulled in one direction toward Special Education and at the same time I was being pulled to go towards the medical field.

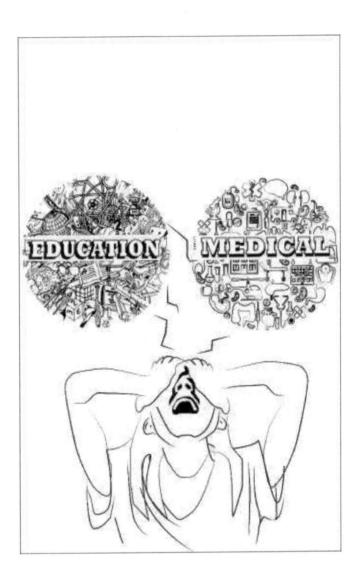

I felt terribly conflicted! So, I did what anyone else would do when they feel torn between decisions, I called my mom. When Mom answered the phone, I asked her how things were going, she replied that everything was fine. She then asked me how school was going, and I told her it was okay. By the tone of my voice, my mom could sense that something was bothering me. I was not my normal, happy and hype self when I talked to her. She asked when I would have free time because she wanted to visit and talk face to face. When mom arrived at school, she surprised me with a bouquet of beautiful roses. Immediately, I thanked her and held her tight. She kissed me on my cheek and said, "Let's take a walk and talk." We took a walk around the soccer field by my dormitory. It was a huge grass field that was bordered by brick walkways, three dormitories, and a building where the hospitality and management majors had many of their classes. As we walked, I told my mom about the tug of war I felt inside of me with wanting to have a career in the medical field and wanting to go into Special

Education. My mom told me that it was my life and that I had to be happy and satisfied with whatever decision I made. "Jamilah, do what will make you happy. Yes, you want to make good money to take care of yourself, but you also want to do something that makes you happy."

After talking with my mom and praying about my conflict, I felt a stronger desire to pursue my degree in Special Education. It was at that moment when I started feeling a stronger pull for me to study Special Education versus a tug toward the medical field. I stopped fighting that tug of war battle going on inside me and made the decision to become a Special Education teacher.

As I began exploring the world of Special Education, I shared information with my mom to help with Aasiyah. I shared things to observe and ask at my sister's Individualized Education Plan (IEP) meetings. An IEP is an educational plan that consists of goals, services, and specific instructions to help a person with a disability reach their goals. I remember a time when my mom didn't sign my sisters IEP and brought it home so that I could look over it. To this day, I do my best to attend all meetings regarding my sister Aasiyah. However, I can't help but think if I am doing enough.

There were times when I would get sad thinking about Aasiyah. She can't just call-up a friend and hang out on her own. My friends are her friends. My mom's friends are her friends. For instance, when my friends are around, Aasiyah joins in on our conversations. She will converse with them individually, asking about their families and how they are doing. The same is with my mom's friends. Aasiyah will go to different community events with one of my mom's friends to just hang out. Our friends are aware of Aasiyah's disability, but they treat her like any other person.

Aasiyah's limitations are still prevalent. She continues to struggle with tying her shoes, reading, and managing money. She also struggles with comprehending certain things, she can't drive a car, or navigate her way through town independently. Sometimes I cry thinking about my sister's limitations. But then I say to myself, "it could be worse." My sister can see, hear, and speak. She can hold a basic conversation with anyone that she encounters. She can give herself her insulin (she has type one diabetes) and she is able to groom herself. Aasiyah also understands that there are consequences for her actions if she does something bad. For example, one day as we were watching the news, an anchorman reported that a man robbed a store. Before the anchorman finished reporting the story, Aasiyah immediately said, "He is going to jail!" Another time, Aasiyah took something that belonged to me and hid it in her room. Our mom found it, talked with her about what she had done, and how it was wrong. She was placed on a brief punishment, and from then on Aasiyah knew if she did something that she shouldn't, there would be a consequence. Aasiyah catches on to routines well and sees the good in everyone. Yes, she still struggles with things. When I see her getting overwhelmed I go to her, gently grab her hands, and tell her to slow down and take a deep breath. Then,

I will ask her if she needs a hug. She will tell me yes or no, then I will ask her what she needs help with and remind her that it is okay to ask for help. One of the best things my mother did for Aasiyah was never allowing her to use her disability as a crutch, i.e. expect and assume that people will automatically come to her aid or excuse certain behaviors exhibited from her. My family and I hold her accountable. Therefore, sometimes we will watch her struggle, teaching her to ask for assistance. When she notices that we are watching her, often she will stop and ask for help. Above all things, my sister has so much confidence and high self-esteem that I wish I could bottle some of it for myself. Things could be so much worse for her, but they aren't and that makes me smile.

I am blessed that Aasiyah is in my life. She has been the driving force of my career in Special Education. It is because of her I have a career that I take much pride in. It is because of Aasiyah I have gone on to further my education to continue to help individuals like her achieve their fullest potential. I am forever thankful for my sister. She has had a tremendous impact on my life. I don't know where I would be without my little sister, Aasiyah. She brings much joy to my life and I literally will act a fool for her just to make her laugh. We love watching comedy movies and she often asks me to reenact parts from her favorite movies and imitate the characters. For her, I mimic the voices and movements of the characters from her favorite scenes of the movies. When I'm done she's normally on the floor in tears from laughing. One of our favorite animated movies is Shrek. We both love the character Donkey. I always reenact the scene where Donkey first sees Shrek's house and insults it. I can't get through reenacting that scene without laughing as Aasiyah is laughing before I can finish the scene.

Those special moments are what makes Aasiyah so special to me. Aasiyah's Honest Exceptional Resilience (H.E.R.) is why I do what I do. Her Honesty is refreshing and annoying sometimes. If you ask her a question or ask for her opinion, she will give it to you whether you like what she says or not and with a smile. What makes Aasiyah an Exceptional person? Aasiyah is a one of a kind being and like no one I have ever known. She is in her own lane, unapologetically. Aasiyah's resilience to overcome adversities in her life has been phenomenal. Having limitations and still capable of living a good quality of life is amazing. At times when I feel overwhelmed and ready to complain, I think about Aasiyah and her daily struggles, i.e. needing assistance with meal preparation, going shopping, and monitoring her diabetes. If she can live a good quality of life with her difficulties and be happy, what am I complaining about. Because of H.E.R. I am reminded of how blessed I am and how I don't have those limitations, but I am devoted to helping those with limitations to reach their fullest potential. It is all Because of H.E.R.

Presently, Aasiyah is twenty-six years old and works at PATH (People Acting to Help). PATH is a mental health agency that provides support to individuals with disabilities through their services for behavioral health and intellectual disabilities. She has an active social life that includes going to community and city events with a friend of our family. She regularly attends Zumba class with our mom at the Kroc Center and sometimes will lead me in my own personal Zumba class. In addition, we still crack each other up with reenacting scenes from our favorite comedy movies.

Aasiyah does enjoy her alone time and does not like for you to plan her time without her consent. She still has her limitations and continues being stubborn when asking for assistance. However, I am learning to give her space to reflect and come to me on her own for help. Looking back to the day my parents brought her home and how excited I was to meet her, but also disappointed that I had a little sister instead of a brother, to now watch her grow into adulthood is bittersweet for me. It is great to see her interacting in an environment where she can be herself and flourish. I can relax more and not hover over her as much. However, I wonder sometimes will she get to a point where she doesn't rely on me as much and no longer needs me. Because of H.E.R., I have no worries. I am in a place where I can step back and watch her come into her own. It is refreshing to witness her growth as a person. She is no longer just my "little sister," she is Aasiyah, my best friend.

73380314R00027

Made in the
USA
Middletown, DE